THIS CANDLEWICK BOOK BELONGS TO:

_____

_____

_____

READ AND WONDER

BIG ANIMALS

CANDLEWICK PRESS
CAMBRIDGE, MASSACHUSETTS

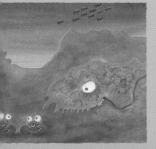

CONTENTS

ABOUT ELEPHANTS

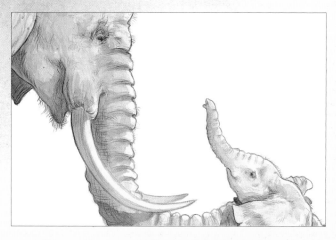

There are two kinds of living elephants. The elephants in this book are African elephants; the other kind are Asian elephants, which live in South and Southeast Asia. Elephants were once found almost everywhere in Africa, but now they have disappeared from many of the places where they used to live. This is because they have been hunted and people have taken their land for farming. Twenty years ago, there were more than one million African elephants. Now there may be only half that number.

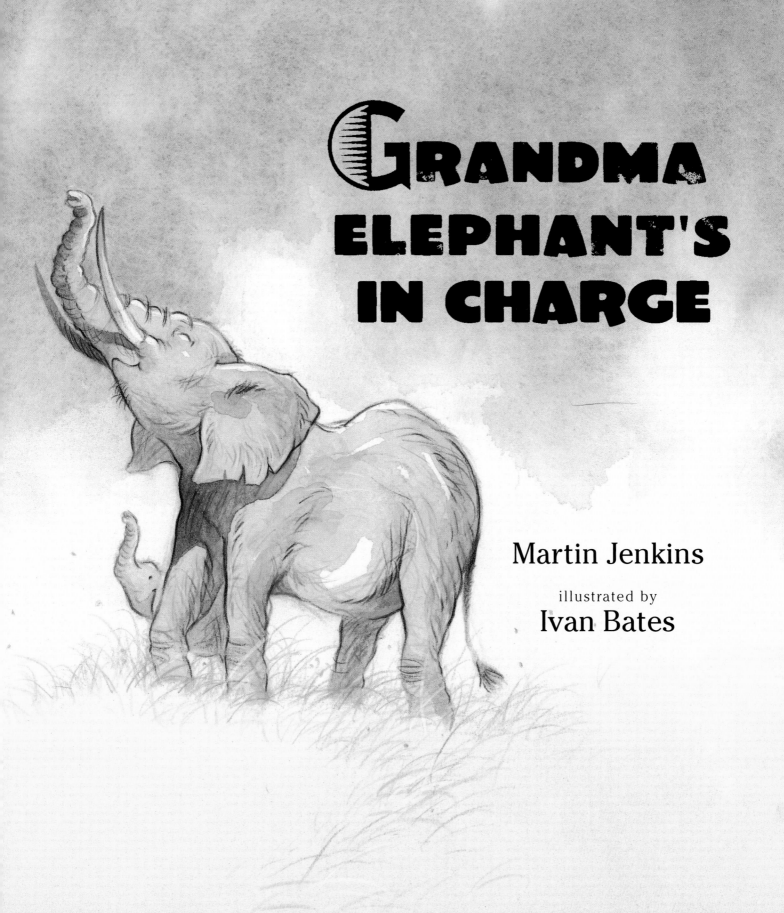

GRANDMA ELEPHANT'S IN CHARGE

Martin Jenkins

illustrated by
Ivan Bates

Most elephants live in families.
And most elephant
families are **big**
(just like elephants).

Elephants are the biggest land
animals of all. A big male
can weigh six tons—
as much as 100 people.

11

There'll probably be two or three babies,
forever playing push-me-pull-you, or peekaboo,
or anything else that makes a lot of noise.
And each of the babies might have an older brother
or sister—handy for playing king-of-the-mountain on!

Elephant mothers have only one baby at a time.
They give birth every three or four years.
Elephants don't become fully grown until
they're ten years old or more.

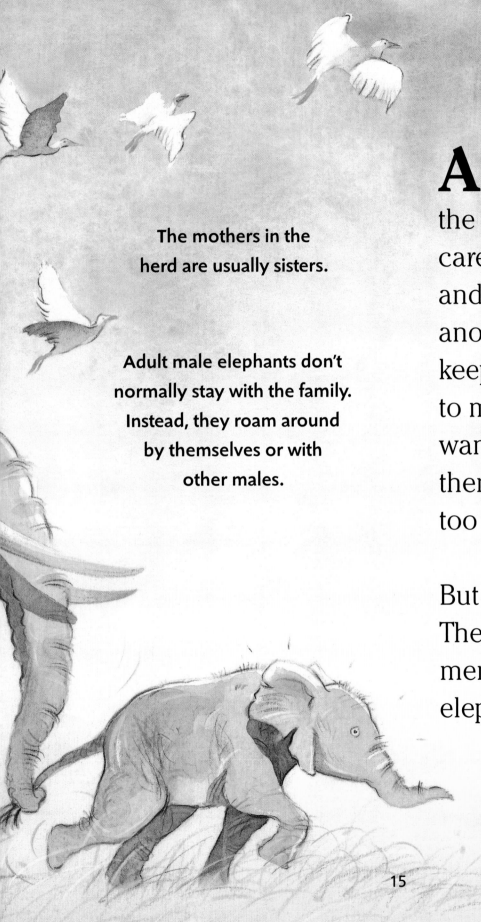

The mothers in the
herd are usually sisters.

Adult male elephants don't
normally stay with the family.
Instead, they roam around
by themselves or with
other males.

And then there are
the moms. They take
care of their own babies
and help with one
another's too—
keeping an eye on them
to make sure they don't
wander off, and scolding
them when they get
too boisterous.

But that's not all.
The most important
member of an
elephant family is...

Grandma!

Elephants can live for up to sixty-five years but don't usually have any more babies once they're older than fifty or so.

Grandma's been around a long time and she knows lots of important things. She knows where the water holes are when it hasn't rained and the easiest places to cross the big river when it has rained.

Elephants move around a lot.
It's important for them to have good
memories so that the family doesn't get
lost when they return to
places they haven't visited
for a very long time.

She knows where to find the juiciest melons. . .
and knows the best path up the cliff to the salt lick.
It's not surprising that she's the one in charge.

Elephants are very fond of things like melons but feed mainly on grass, leaves, and twigs. Adults eat about 350 pounds of food each day.

Salt licks are places where the earth is full of minerals. Lots of animals eat the salty earth there, which helps to keep them healthy.

She doesn't make a big song and dance about it, though. Just a flick of the ear or a snort or two, and a **rumble, rumble, rumble,** deep down in her throat, seem to be enough to tell all the other elephants what to do.

If she stops, they all stop. If she moves, they all move. And if there's any sign of danger, you can be sure she'll be the first to investigate and the first to decide what the family should do.

They might all run away...
or they might take a stand.

Or Grandma might **c-h-a-r-g-e**.
If she charges with her head up and ears
flapping, waving her trunk and making
a great hullabaloo, then she's probably
bluffing.

But if her head's down, her trunk's
tucked under, and she's not making
any noise, then she means business.
In that case, whoever it is that has
annoyed her had better watch out.

**A charging elephant can
run at 25 miles an hour — that's faster
than the fastest human.**

And once all the commotion's over,
everyone can settle back down to feeding
and snoozing and messing around—
knowing that Grandma has sorted things
out again.

So if you're an elephant, there's one thing you should never forget. Wherever you are and whatever you're doing,

Grandma's in charge!

About pandas

Giant pandas live in just a few high
mountain forests in southwest China.
Because female pandas raise just one cub
at a time, panda numbers are slow to grow.
It does not help that poachers still hunt
them and loggers threaten their habitat.
Where special reserves are set up
to protect them, pandas do well. Even so,
their future survival is at risk: there are
only about 2,500 wild giant pandas left.

Tracks of a PANDA

Nick Dowson illustrated by Yu Rong

High on a
mist-wrapped mountain,
cradled in a leafy nest,
Panda holds her newborn cub
gently in her giant paw.

Small as a pinecone,
pink as a blob of
wriggling sunset,
he sinks, squawking, into
his mother's fur
until her warm milk
fills his mouth.

Panda cubs
are born blind
and almost
furless.
They are
900 times
smaller than
their mothers.

For days Panda stays with her cub

in their hollow tree den.

But the need to feed herself

grows stronger, and

one bright August morning

she leaves him and

follows her old tracks

to the patch of

bamboo grass where she eats.

There are many
different kinds
of bamboo,
but pandas
usually choose
to eat only
a few kinds.

Pandas have
very big
back teeth
to help them
crush tough
bamboo stems.

She rolls on her back in
a soft bed of ferns and grabs a
handful of bamboo.
Slowly her big black nose wrinkles:
these leaves smell good
and she is very hungry.
Before she goes back to cuddle
and suckle her cub,
Panda strips
ten stems bare.

For seven weeks the cub's eyes stay shut.
He feeds and sleeps, cries and gurgles.
As he grows, around his ears and eyes,
across his legs, and like a road of
hairy ink on his back,
some of his fur
darkens, like his
mom's, into black.

One fall day, he crawls up Panda's chest
onto her neck. Something cold and wet
tickles his nose, and his eyes open for the
first time—onto a world of falling snow.

It takes four years for panda cubs to be as big as their mothers.

The cub grows fast through winter.
He still climbs and plays on his mother, but now he also takes
his first steps along the mountain tracks.

But Panda has not eaten well for weeks.
Her bamboo patch is dying. Now that her cub is
six months old and strong enough to travel,
she knows they must find a new home.

Pandas' black and white fur is good camouflage in winter.

Below her old territory,
the path is steep.
Weak with hunger,
Panda stumbles
and bumps her cub into
a deep drift of snow.

She goes to him and
smells an unexpected
buried meal there.
Snow flies as she scrapes.
This deer meat is old
but will give her strength.

Pandas almost always
eat bamboo, but they
sometimes eat other
things — such as
insects, fish, or meat.

44

After eating, Panda
suckles her sleepy cub,
then, thirsty, drinks
from a stream.

A shadow slips through
the trees. Closer it comes,
its long tongue lolling.

Panda lifts her big
dripping head.
Like knives, her long
claws slash the air,
and the wild dog growls
and slinks away.

When they
need to defend
their cubs,
mother pandas
are very fierce.

47

With danger in the forest,
Panda needs a safe
place to sleep:
in a tree.

48

She hugs the fir's frosty
trunk with both arms, and
her strong claws and
furry feet grip the bark.
Her cub clings to her
shoulder as they clamber
toward the clouds;
then he leaves
her and scrambles
to his own high perch.

Like other bears,
pandas are very
good climbers.

49

When she wakes, Panda suckles her cub but
still needs food for herself. They move on.

Soon she sees a new mountain rising,
with bamboo on its slopes.
Cold water laps at her tired feet,
and she walks into a
stream's dark pool.

To move from
place to place
in the mountains,
pandas need to
be able to swim.

50

Her paws touch bottom all the way, but in the middle
the cub has to swim. He kicks hard with his feet,
and his paws turn to paddles as he pushes the
water behind him.

Pandas have five "fingers," plus a sixth one, more like a thumb, that helps them hold bamboo.

This new territory
has plenty of food.
Panda won't go hungry now.
Her cub, too,
begins to eat bamboo.
He grips a stem and,
copying his mother,
curls his sticky tongue
around the leaves.

Spring brings warm rain, and juicy
new shoots of bamboo poke up.
One day, mother and cub are
feeding when they hear axes thud
and branches crash nearby.
Panda stops chewing.
Villagers are chopping firewood.
If they move up the mountain,
she and her cub cannot stay.
Slowly she climbs up a deer path,
her cub close behind…

Mother pandas
will not share
territory with
other pandas
or people.

54

Clouds curl around their tracks as they go.
Their hunt for a new home is beginning again.

About Blue Whales

For every blue whale alive today
there were once twenty.
People hunted and killed so many of them
that fewer than 10,000 remain.
Now blue whales are protected
and hunting them is banned,
so in some places their numbers are
growing—very, very slowly.
Still, you could sail the oceans for a year
and never see a single one.

BIG BLUE
WHALE

NICOLA DAVIES

illustrated by NICK MALAND

The blue whale is big.

Bigger than a giraffe.

Bigger than an elephant.

Bigger than a dinosaur.

The blue whale is
the biggest creature
that has ever lived
on Earth!

Female blue whales are a little bigger than the males.

Blue whales can grow to 100 feet long and weigh 150 tons—that's heavier than 25 elephants or 115 giraffes.

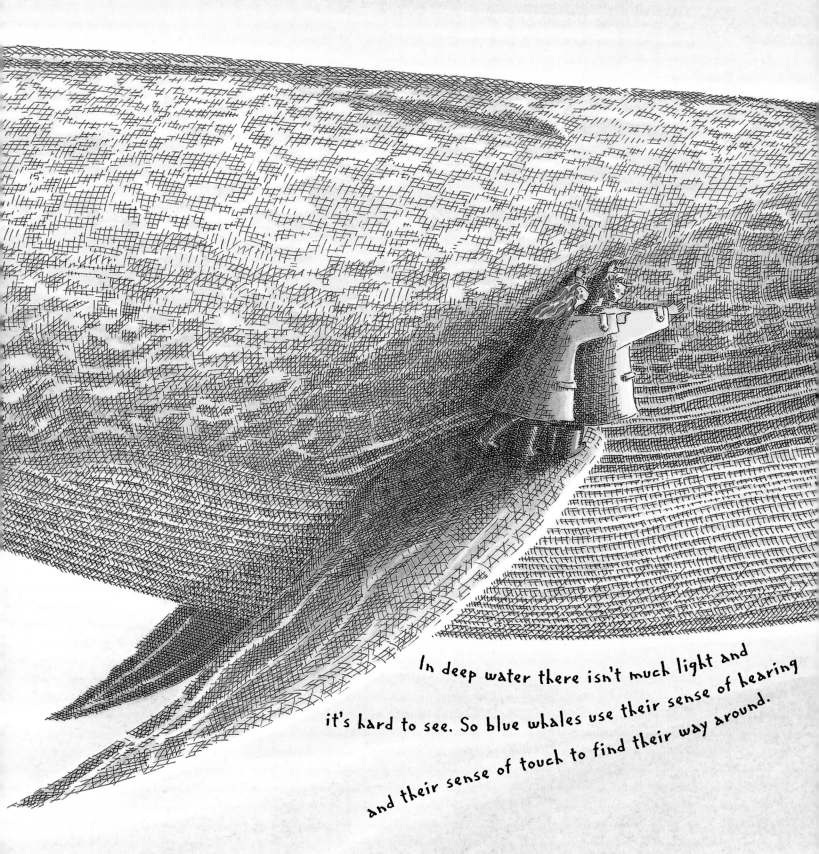

In deep water there isn't much light and it's hard to see. So blue whales use their sense of hearing and their sense of touch to find their way around.

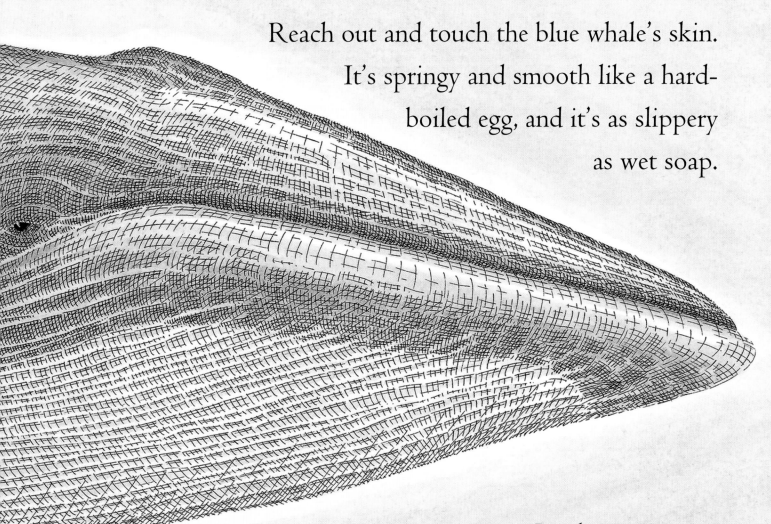

Reach out and touch the blue whale's skin.
It's springy and smooth like a hard-
boiled egg, and it's as slippery
as wet soap.

Look into its eye.
It's as big as a teacup and as dark
as the deep sea. Just behind the eye is a hole
as small as the end of a pencil. The hole is one of
the blue whale's ears—sticking-out ears would
get in the way when the whale is swimming.

The blue whale lives all of its long life in the sea.
But it is a mammal like us, and it breathes air, not water.

From time to time, it has to come to the surface to breathe
through the blowholes on top of its head.

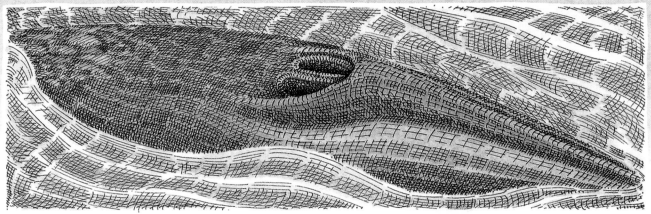

Blue whales can live for about 70 to 80 years.

When it breathes out,
it makes a great misty puff
as high as a house.
This is the whale's blow,
and you can see it from far away.
You can hear it, too—a great

PROOUFF.

And if you are close enough
you can smell it, as the whale's
breath is stale and fishy.

A blue whale can stay underwater for 30 minutes or more.
But on long journeys, it usually surfaces for air every 2 to 5 minutes.

A blue whale can have
as many as 790 baleen plates in its mouth.
Baleen is tough bendy stuff, like extra-hard fingernails.

Take a look inside its mouth. Don't worry,
the blue whale doesn't eat people.
It doesn't even have any teeth. It has
hundreds of baleen plates instead.
They're the long bristly things
hanging down from its top jaw.

The whale doesn't need teeth for biting
or chewing, because its food is tiny!

The blue whale
eats krill—pale pinkish
shrimplike creatures the size
of your little finger.

Billions of them live
in the cold seas around
the North and South Poles.
in summer there can be so many
that the water looks pink—
so that's when the blue whales
come to the polar seas to eat.
It takes an awful lot of
tiny krill to feed
a great big blue whale.
But the whale doesn't catch
them one at a time.
It has a special way of
swallowing whole swarms
of them at once.

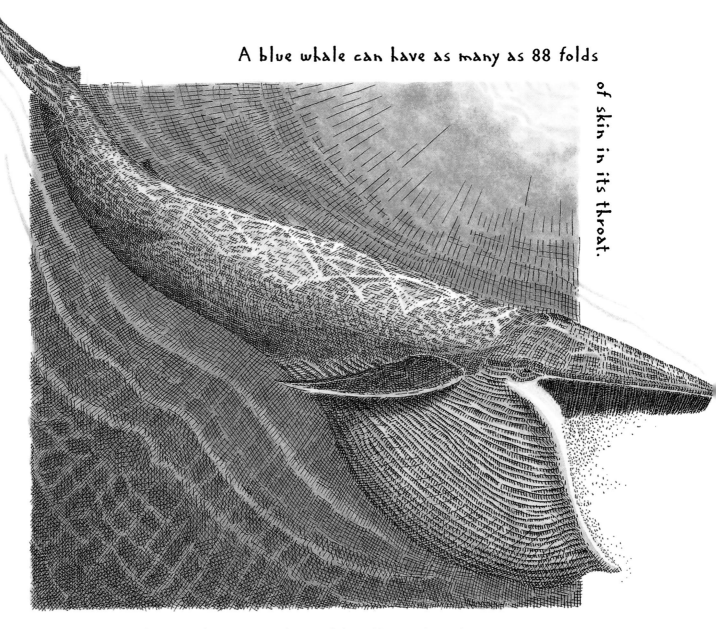

A blue whale can have as many as 88 folds of skin in its throat.

First, it takes a huge gulp of krill and salty seawater. There's room for all this because the whale's throat unfolds and opens out like a vast balloon. Then it uses its big tongue to push the water out between its bristly baleen plates.

The water streams away and leaves the krill caught
on the bristles like peas in a sieve.
Now all the whale has to do is lick them
off and swallow them.

A blue whale can eat about 30 million krill just in one day—that's three big truckloads!

And this is how the blue whale spends the summer—
eating krill and getting fat. But in the fall,
the polar seas freeze over.

In summer, the blue whale grows a thick layer of fat all over its body. This fat is called blubber, and it's a food store for the winter, when the whale eats very little.

The krill hide under the ice where the whale cannot catch them. So, the whale swims away from the icy cold and winter storms.

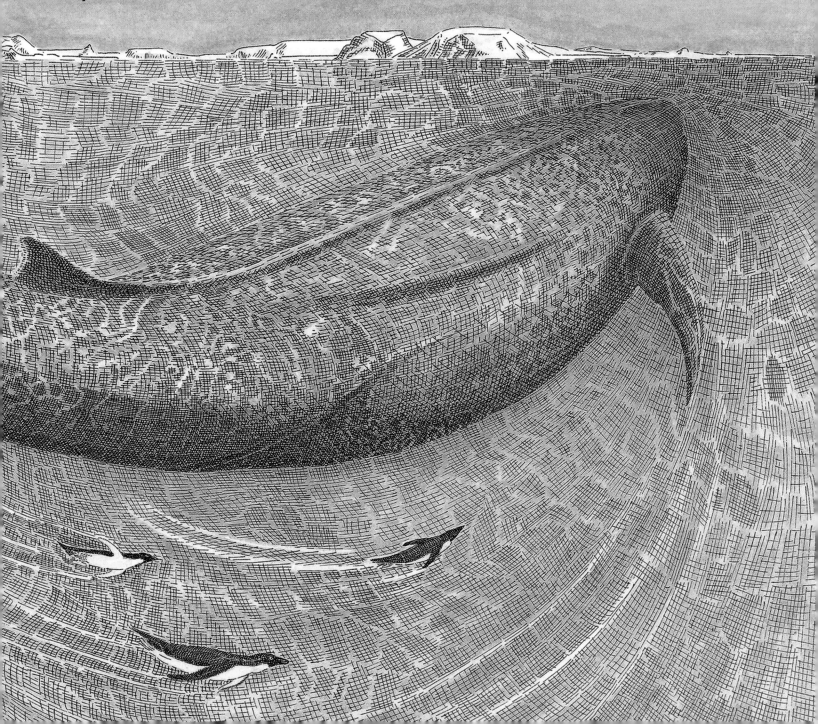

Day after day, the blue whale swims slowly and steadily toward its winter home. Its huge tail beats up and down to push it along. Its flippers steer it left or right.

For two months and more the whale swims, until at last it reaches the calm warm seas near the equator.

There it stays all winter.

Some blue whales spend their summers around the South Pole and swim north to the equator for the winter.

Others live around the North Pole and swim south for the winter.

North Pole

Atlantic
Ocean

Equator

Atlantic
Ocean

But when it's winter at the
South Pole, it's summer
at the North Pole.

So the two groups
of whales never meet.

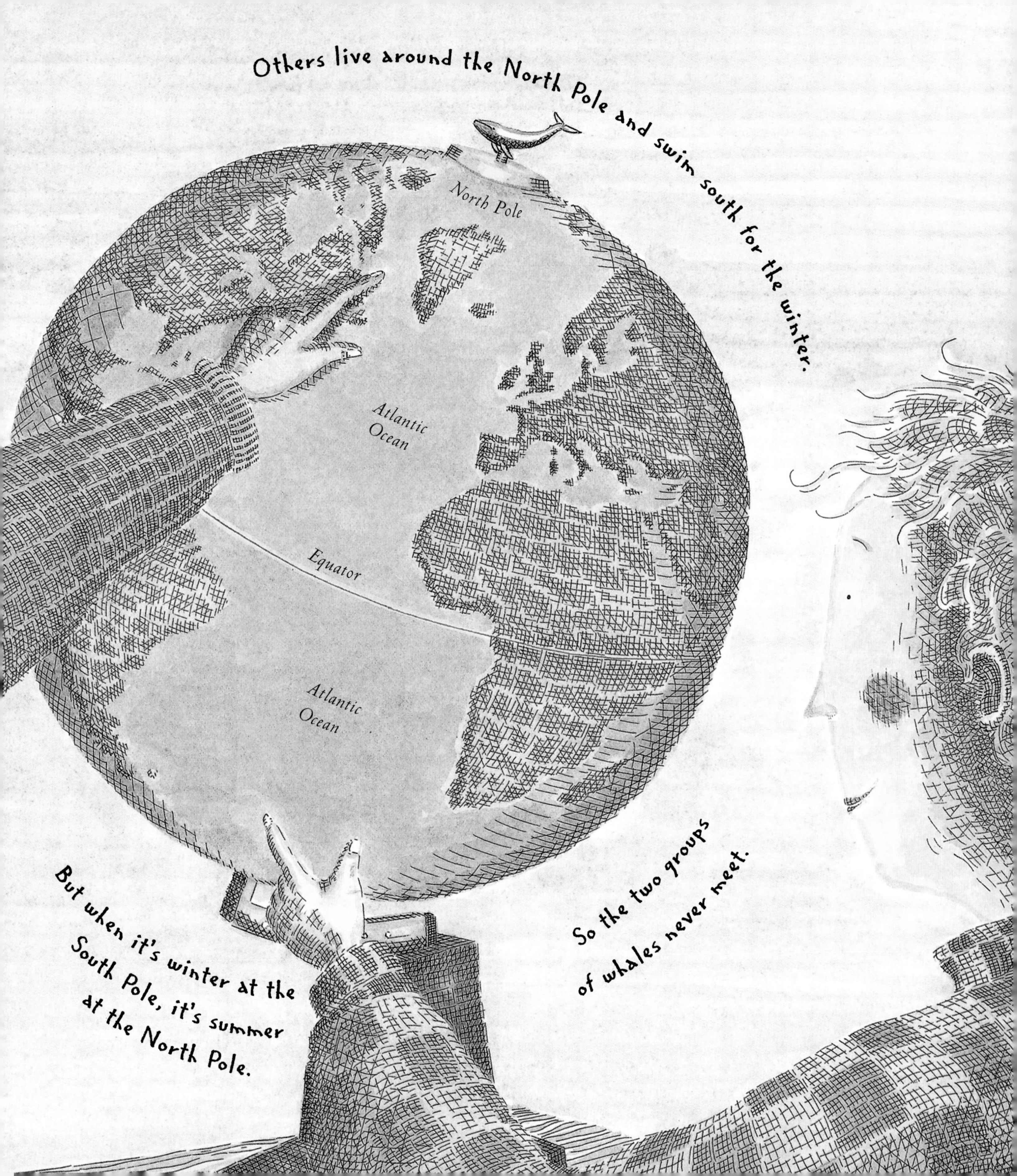

And there the blue whale mother gives birth to her baby,
where storms and cold weather can't hurt it.

Male and female blue whales mate in winter and then part.
Babies are born about a year later.

The blue whale's baby slithers from her body, tail first.

Gently she nudges it to the surface to take its first breath.

Then the baby dives beneath her to take its first drink of milk.

A blue whale baby is 23 feet long at birth. It drinks more than 150 gallons of milk a day, suckling it from the teats tucked into its mother's belly.

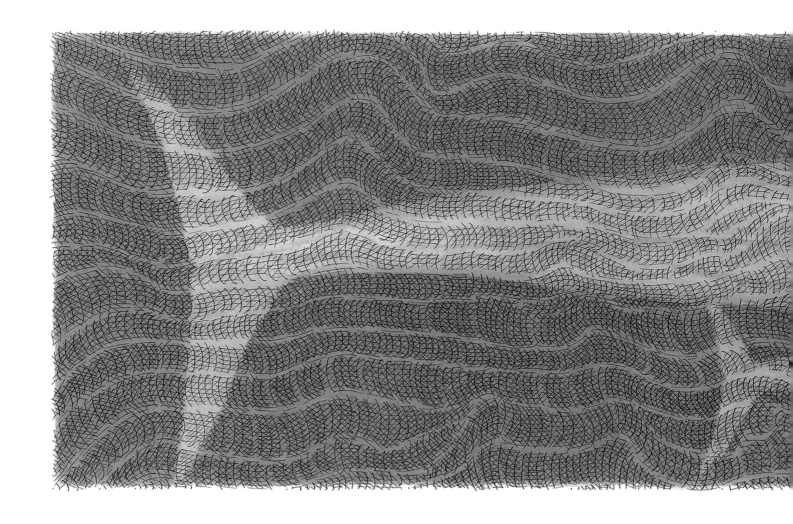

All through the winter, the blue whale keeps
her baby close. It feeds on her creamy milk,
and it grows and grows.
In spring, the two whales return to the polar seas
to feast on krill together. But by the fall,
the young whale is big enough to live on its own.

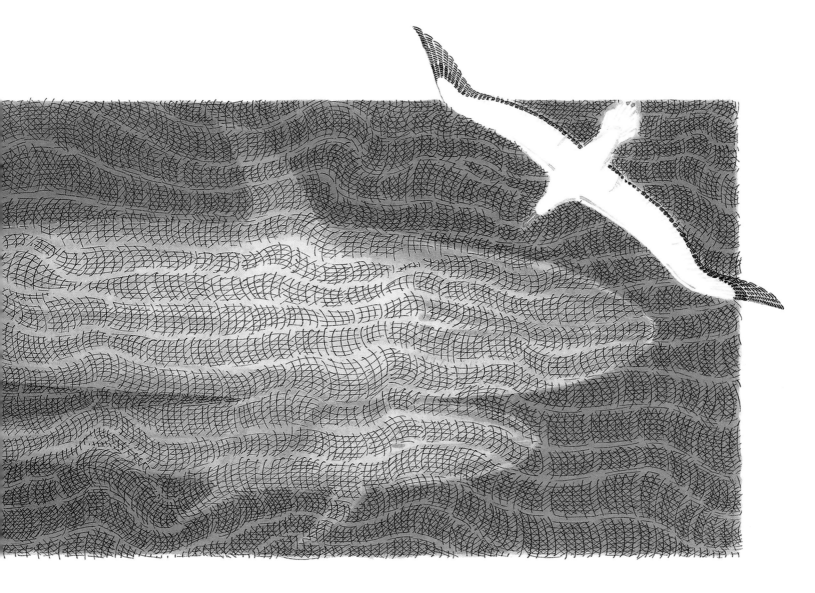

So mother and young whale part and begin
the long journey back to the equator.
A blue whale may travel from the polar seas
to the equator and back every year of its life.
Sometimes it will swim with other blue whales,
but mostly it will swim alone.

Adult blue whales make their hums in deep water. It's much cooler than near the surface, which helps the hum to travel a long way.

Yet, the blue whale may not be
as lonely as it seems.
Because sometimes it makes
a hum—a hum so loud and
so low that it can travel for
thousands of miles through the
seas to reach other blue whales.
Only a very low hum could travel
so far. And only a very big animal
could make a hum so low.
Perhaps that's why blue whales
are the biggest creatures
on Earth—so that they can
talk to one another even when
they are far apart.
Who knows what they say.
"Here I am!" would be enough...

because in
the vastness
of the green seas,
even a blue whale is small—
and hard to find.

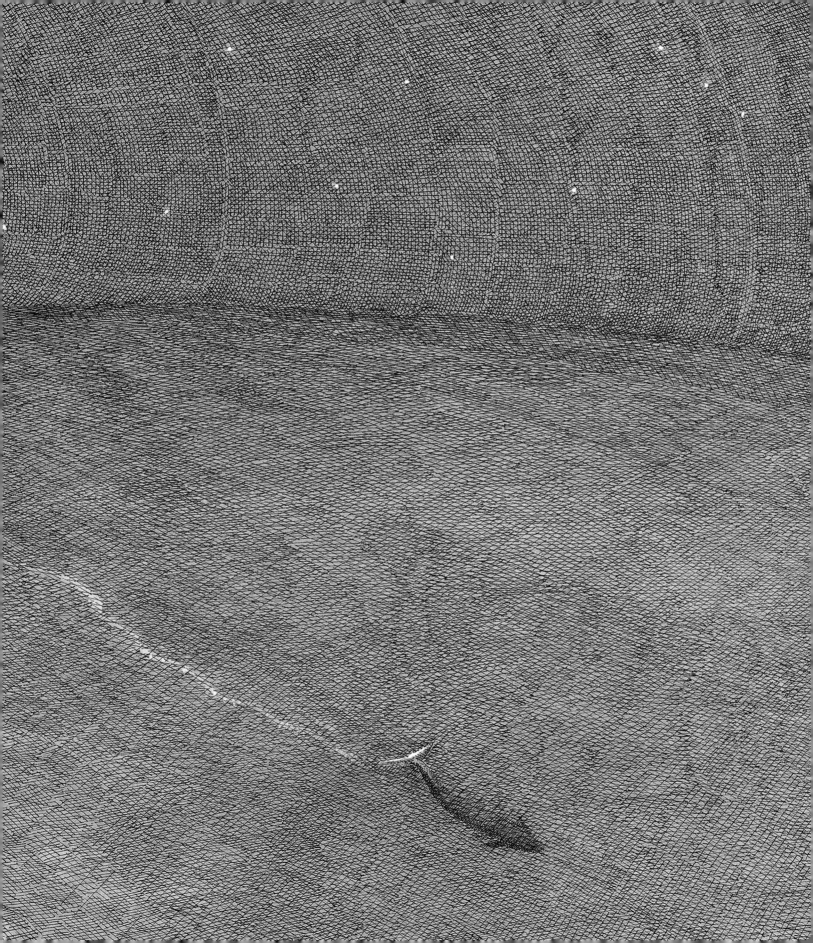

About Tigers

For years, tigers were hunted and killed in large numbers, and of the eight kinds that once prowled the forests, only five survive. There are fewer than 6,000 tigers alive today, scattered across parts of China, Indonesia, India, and southeastern Russia.

Today tigers are protected, but poachers do still kill them. And people are slowly moving into the land where they live, threatening our last wild tigers with extinction.

Tigress

Nick Dowson

illustrated by Jane Chapman

Twigs with whiskers?

A tree with a tail?

Or is it a tigress,

hiding?

Tigers are rarely seen, even though they can grow as big as Shetland ponies. Tigers' bright stripes are perfect camouflage in their natural surroundings.

She can look exactly like a patch of forest, just by being there.
When she stalks slowly through leaves and shadows,
or crouches still in elephant grass,
her fiery, stripy coat seems to vanish

like magic.

Bigger than your fist,
her pink nose sniffs the air.

Her ears turn to listen
for the smallest noise.

Bright as torches,
her large yellow eyes
gleam all around.

Tigers don't have a great sense of smell, but their eyesight is six times better than ours, and they have amazing hearing.

She's searching for a new den.

Somewhere safe for young cubs.

87

Smooth as a river she moves.
Her plate-size paws press the ground
but don't make a sound.
When she runs, strong muscles stretch
and ripple her body like wind on water.

She finds an untidy pile of rocks across the clearing,
full of dark cracks and crevices.
Perfect hiding for tiny cubs.

She will bring them here tonight.

Mother tigers look after their cubs alone.
So when the mothers hunt, the cubs are left unprotected.
Changing dens helps to fool predators, such as leopards
and wild dogs, that may kill the cubs.

Back at the old den, the cubs are snuggled deep in shaded sleep.

Their bright white ear spots wink like magic eyes.

With rough, wet licks from her long tongue, the tigress stirs them awake.

No one knows for sure why tigers have ear spots.
They may help small cubs to follow their mother.
Or perhaps they are flashed as
a warning to other tigers.

Grooming keeps their fur sleek and clean, but the wriggling cubs are eager to feed.

Weighing only a few pounds, baby tigers drink rich mother's milk

and fill up like fat, furry cushions.

These two are too small to walk far, so the tigress uses tooth power.

The gentle mother carries her dangling cubs, one by one,

to safety at the new den.

Tiger cubs have loose skin on
their necks, which makes
them easy to lift.

93

While the tigress hunts for food,
brother and sister stalk,
stretch, and snarl.
Teeth bared, heads together,

this could be a tiger fight.

But their knife-sharp claws are
sheathed this time and don't draw
blood. The cubs are six months
old now—when they are
older, their claws will cut
deep into the hardest wood
or the tough hide of
their prey.

Tigers can get badly hurt in fights,
so they usually avoid each other. Tigers
find their own territory, which they mark
by scratching trees and rocks and by leaving
their scent on bushes and leaves.

95

Sharp grass stems scratch three empty bellies.
For days mother and cubs have chewed old
skin and crunched cold bones.
The tigress needs a big kill, and now
the hungry year-old cubs are too big
and strong to play-hunt by the den.

A wild pig's big, bristly head bends
as his snout shoves and snuffles for grubs.
Fierce eyes burning, noses wrinkling
with his smell, the three tigers creep
closer with soft, slow steps.
They crouch, still as stone.

Young tigers start eating
meat at about eight weeks old.

The cubs' whiskers quiver. Their hearts thump loud as drums.
Like fire, the roaring tigress leaps and falls
in a crush of teeth and muscle.
Mouths wide open, her snarling
cubs rush in.

Tigers are good hunters, but even they catch their prey only three times out of every ten attempts on average. Tiger cubs always eat first, and if there's not much meat, the mother may not feed at all.

Now the family will eat its fill.

The sun turns tiger fur oven-hot,
so after the big feed and a sleep,
the tigress heads for the lake.

While her cubs splash and
swim, she floats in cool,
green water to soak
away the heat.

Tigers are among the few big cats to enjoy swimming.

Between eighteen months and three years old, tigers leave their old territory and find a new territory of their own.

Three sleek tigers prowl the midnight forest.

The tigress has taught the two cubs all her tricks.

Now, at eighteen months, they must find their own homes without her.

A pattern of gliding stripes slides into the trees,
and the mother disappears.
Brother nuzzles sister for the last time and walks away.

She watches the forest swallow his tail.

Then she turns and silently crosses the moonlit clearing.

And just like her magic mother, the young tigress

vanishes.

About Sharks

Sharks have been on Earth
for 300 million years and can
be found today in every
ocean and sea in the world.
People see sharks as
monsters, but of the 500
different kinds of sharks in
the world, only 30 have ever
attacked humans, and most
feed on shellfish and
small fish.

Sharks are predators: they kill
only to eat and are as
important in the sea as
wolves, lions, tigers, and
bears are on land.

SURPRISING SHARKS

Nicola Davies

illustrated by
James Croft

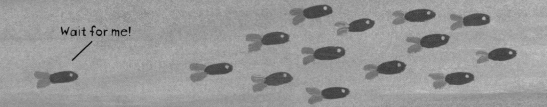

Wait for me!

You're swimming in the warm blue sea.
What's the one word that turns your
dream into a nightmare?

What's the one word that
makes you think of a

giant
man-eating
killer?

Shark? Yes, it's a shark!

It's a **DWARF LANTERN SHARK**.
It's the smallest kind of shark in the world,
just bigger than a chocolate bar. Not a giant,
certainly no man-eater, and a killer only
if you happen to be a shrimp.

You see, **MOST** sharks are not at all what you might expect. After all, who would expect a shark to. . .

Like all **LANTERN SHARKS,** this **BLACKBELLY LANTERN SHARK** has light-making organs on its tummy. They help it to blend in with the silvery surface of the sea and avoid ending up as dinner for bigger fish.

have built-in fairy lights. . .

or blow up like a party balloon. . .

SWELL SHARKS swallow water when they get scared. They blow up to three times their normal size so that they stick fast between rocks. Then no predator can pull them out.

This Australian shark is called a **WOBBEGONG**. Its patterned skin matches the rocks and coral on the seafloor, so it can sneak up on shellfish, crabs, and small fish without being seen.

or lie on the seafloor like a scrap of old carpet...

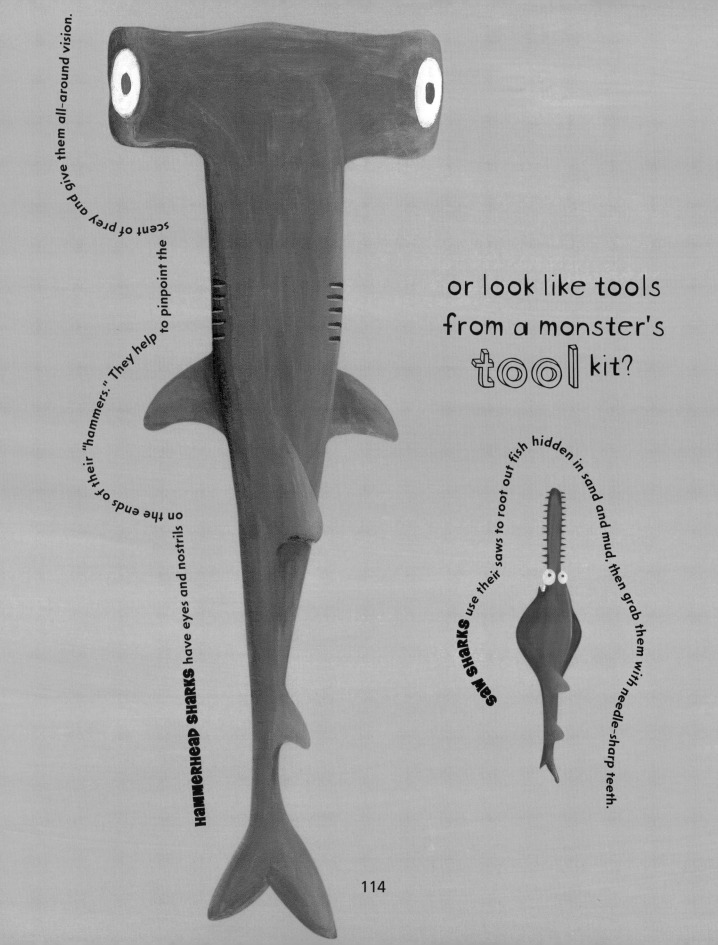

HAMMERHEAD SHARKS have eyes and nostrils on the ends of their "hammers." They help to pinpoint the scent of prey and give them all-around vision.

or look like tools from a monster's tool kit?

SAW SHARKS use their saws to root out fish hidden in sand and mud, then grab them with needle-sharp teeth.

114

In fact, sharks come in all sorts of shapes and sizes.

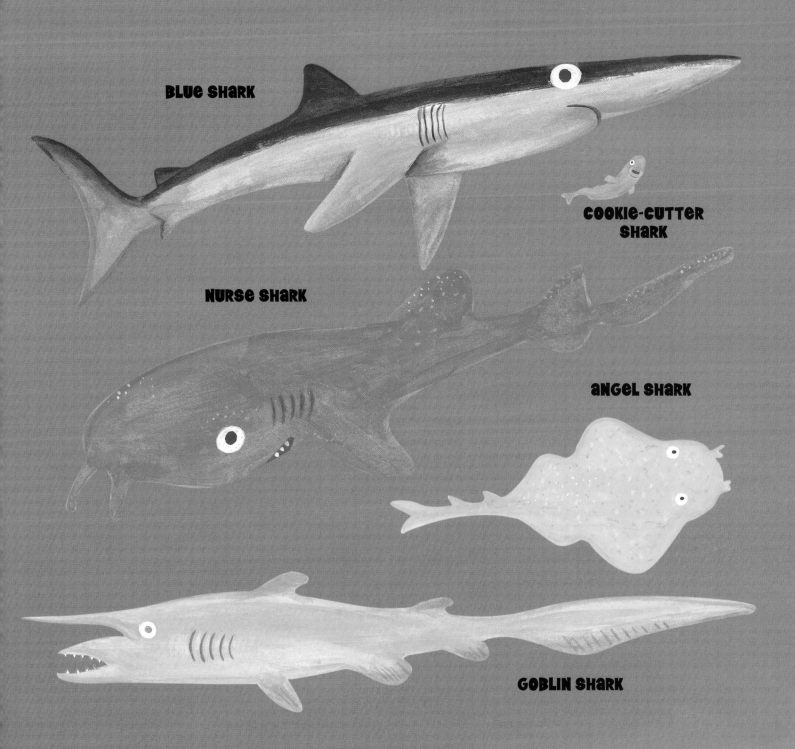

BLUE SHARK

COOKIE-CUTTER SHARK

NURSE SHARK

ANGEL SHARK

GOBLIN SHARK

How can such different animals all be sharks?
Look carefully and you'll see
all the things they share.

DORSAL FIN

TAIL

PELVIC
FIN

FINS AND TAIL FOR SWIMMING...
A shark's tail fins are bigger at the top
than at the bottom, unlike other fish tails.
Their tails push them through the water,
and the fins help them to swim left or right,
up or down.

PECTORAL
FIN

Outside:

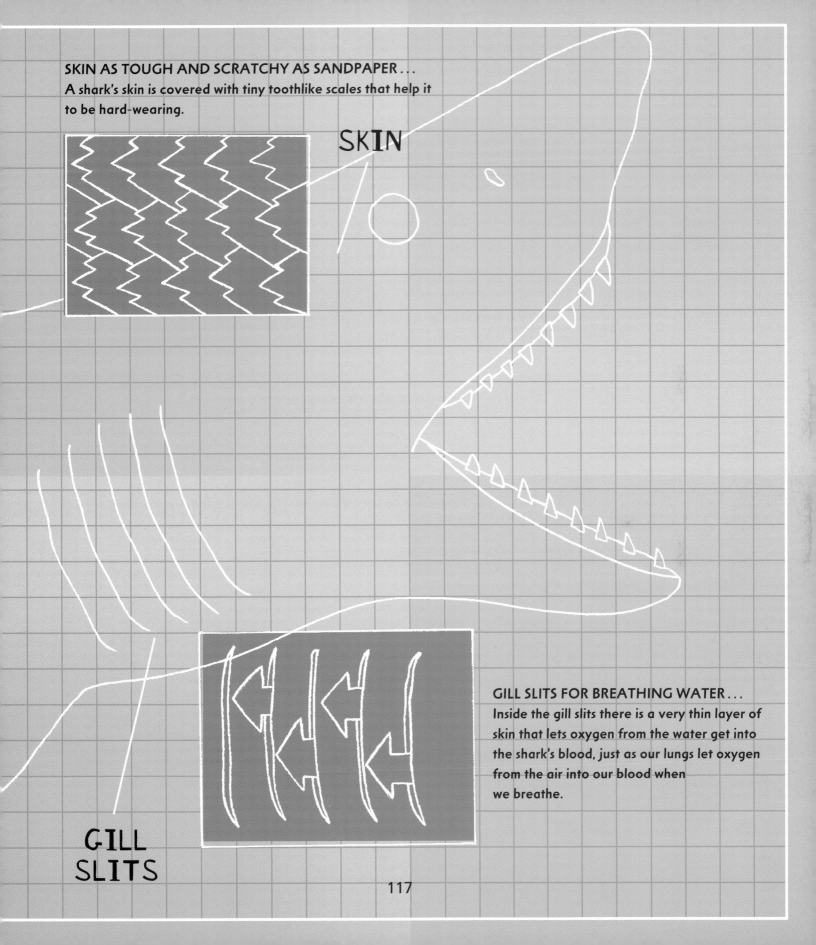

SKIN AS TOUGH AND SCRATCHY AS SANDPAPER...
A shark's skin is covered with tiny toothlike scales that help it
to be hard-wearing.

SKIN

GILL
SLITS

GILL SLITS FOR BREATHING WATER...
Inside the gill slits there is a very thin layer of
skin that lets oxygen from the water get into
the shark's blood, just as our lungs let oxygen
from the air into our blood when
we breathe.

117

Inside:

JAWS THAT CAN POP OUT THROUGH
THE MOUTH LIKE A JACK-IN-THE-BOX...
Sharks' jaws aren't part of their heads as ours are.
Instead, they're held on by a kind of living rubber
band, so the jaws can shoot forward
fast to grab prey.

JAWS

TEETH

ROWS AND ROWS OF SPARE TEETH, SO
THAT THE SHARK IS NEVER WITHOUT ITS BITE...
A shark can have up to 3,000 teeth, all in rows,
one behind the other. As one tooth wears out,
the one behind it moves forward to replace it.
So sharks always have sharp teeth and use
more than 20,000 in their lifetime.

A BENDY, BONELESS SKELETON THAT HELPS STOP IT FROM SINKING...
Shark skeletons are made of the tough kind of stuff that makes up your ears and the end of your nose—cartilage. It floats in water—like a rubber ball.

SKELETON

But it isn't the basic body plan that makes sharks sharks...

119

It's the **sharkish** way they behave!
Sharks are always hungry, and they're
always on the lookout for their next
meal. Some even start **killing**
before they're born.

SAND TIGER SHARKS
give birth to just two
live young — which is all
that's left after those two
have eaten the other six
babies in their mother's belly.

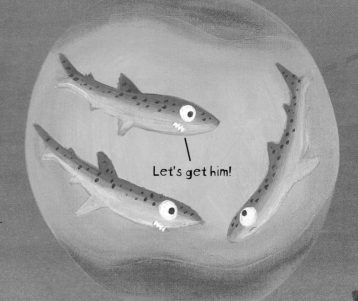

Let's get him!

Some sharks lay eggs, and some give birth to
live young. But all baby sharks are just like
their parents, with **sharp teeth** and
the ability to hunt right from the start.

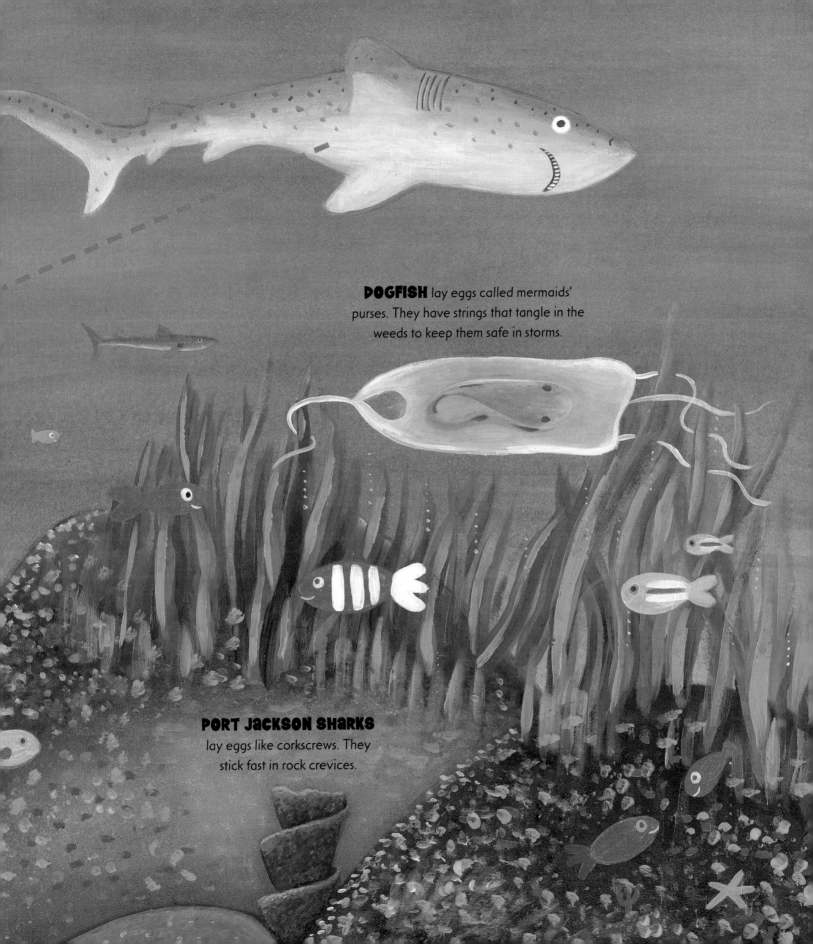

DOGFISH lay eggs called mermaids' purses. They have strings that tangle in the weeds to keep them safe in storms.

PORT JACKSON SHARKS lay eggs like corkscrews. They stick fast in rock crevices.

Sharks' senses are fine-tuned, ready for the tiniest hint that might mean 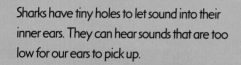!

Sharks have tiny holes to let sound into their inner ears. They can hear sounds that are too low for our ears to pick up.

Sharks' eyes are on the sides of their heads, so they can see almost as well behind them as they can in front!

A shark's skin is sensitive in the same way that your fingertips are. You can tell hot from cold, rough from smooth, moving from still. A shark can also get all sorts of information from the movement and temperature of the water all around its body.

To a hungry shark, the faintest trail of clues is as clear as a restaurant sign.

A shark's nostrils are just under the tip of its snout. Water flows into them as the shark moves forward, bringing any scents with it.

Gel-filled pits in a shark's nose can detect food. Every animal has nerves, which are like cables carrying electrical messages around the body. The shark's gel pits can sense this electricity.

BASKING SHARKS suck in more than 10,000 quarts of plankton-filled water an hour. Plankton is the name for the many kinds of tiny animals and plants that drift around the sea with the wind and tide.

And when at last they're close enough for the kill, they feel the **crackle** of their prey's living nerves, so they bite in just the right place . . . no matter what the prey! Whether it's **plankton** . . .

or **people!** Oh yes, it's true — some sharks do kill people, about six of us every year.

The **GREAT WHITE** is one of just three species of sharks that attack people regularly. The other two are the **BULL SHARK** and the **TIGER SHARK**. In fact, only 30 of the 500 different kinds of sharks have ever attacked humans. Crocodiles, elephants, dogs, and even pigs kill more people every year than sharks do!

But every year **people** kill **100 million** sharks.

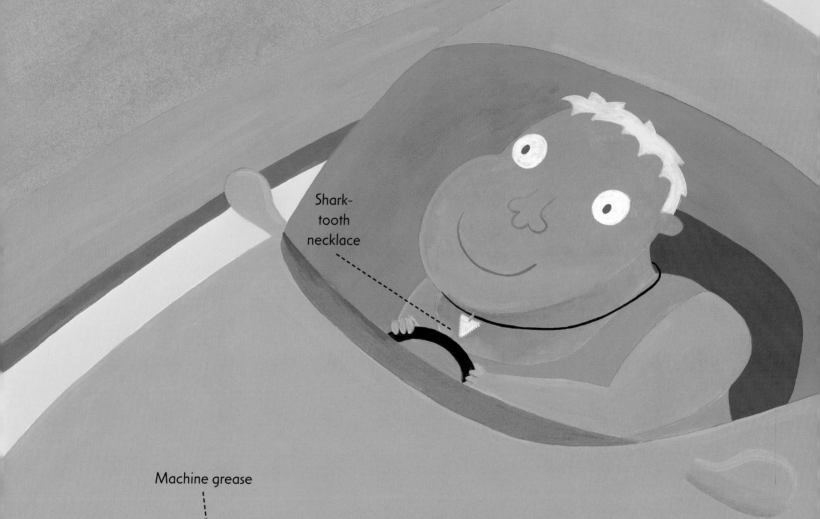

Shark-tooth necklace

Machine grease

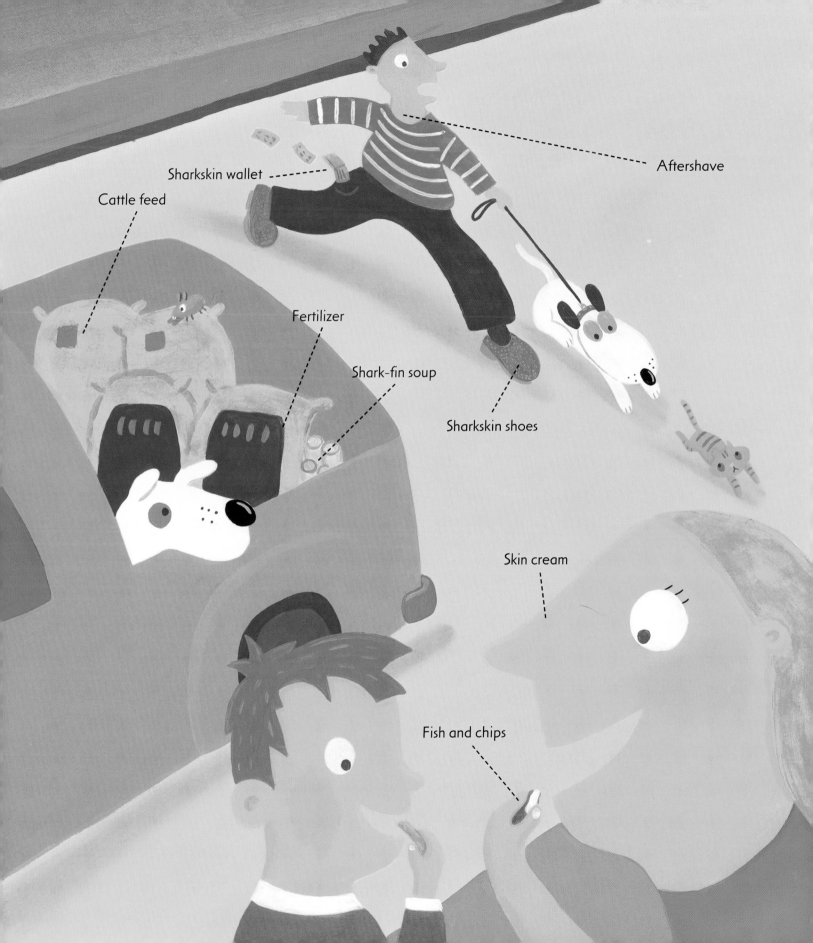

Aftershave

Sharkskin wallet

Cattle feed

Fertilizer

Shark-fin soup

Sharkskin shoes

Skin cream

Fish and chips

If you were a shark swimming in the lovely blue sea, the last word you'd want to hear would be . . .

hUMaN!

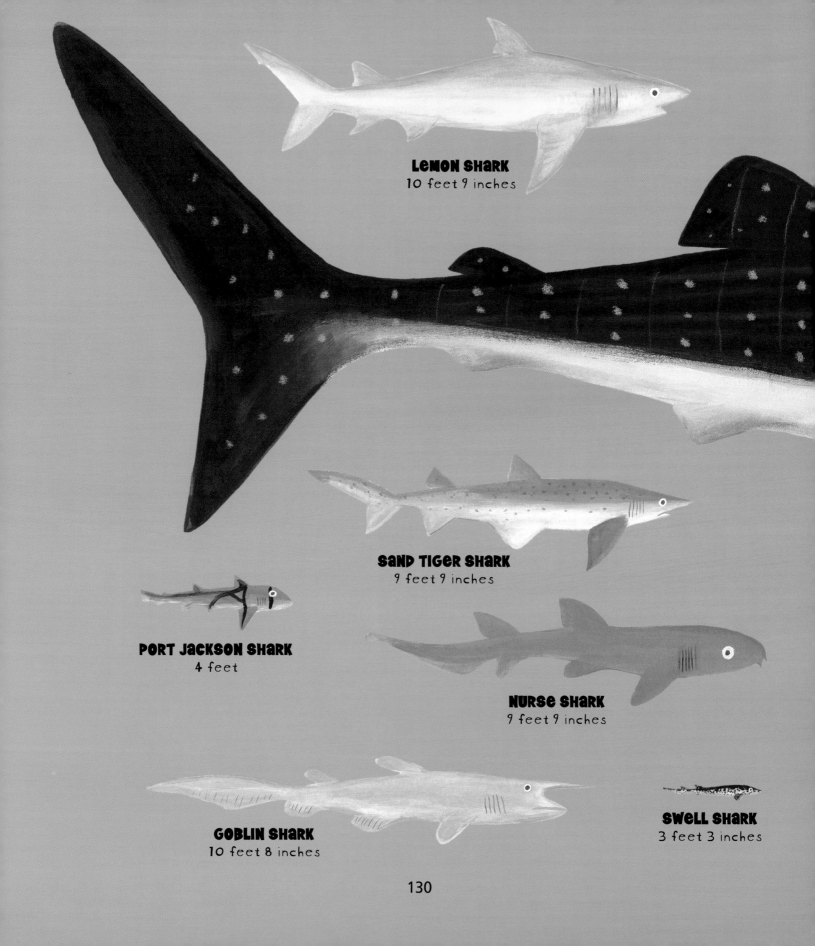

LEMON SHARK
10 feet 9 inches

SAND TIGER SHARK
9 feet 9 inches

PORT JACKSON SHARK
4 feet

NURSE SHARK
9 feet 9 inches

GOBLIN SHARK
10 feet 8 inches

SWELL SHARK
3 feet 3 inches

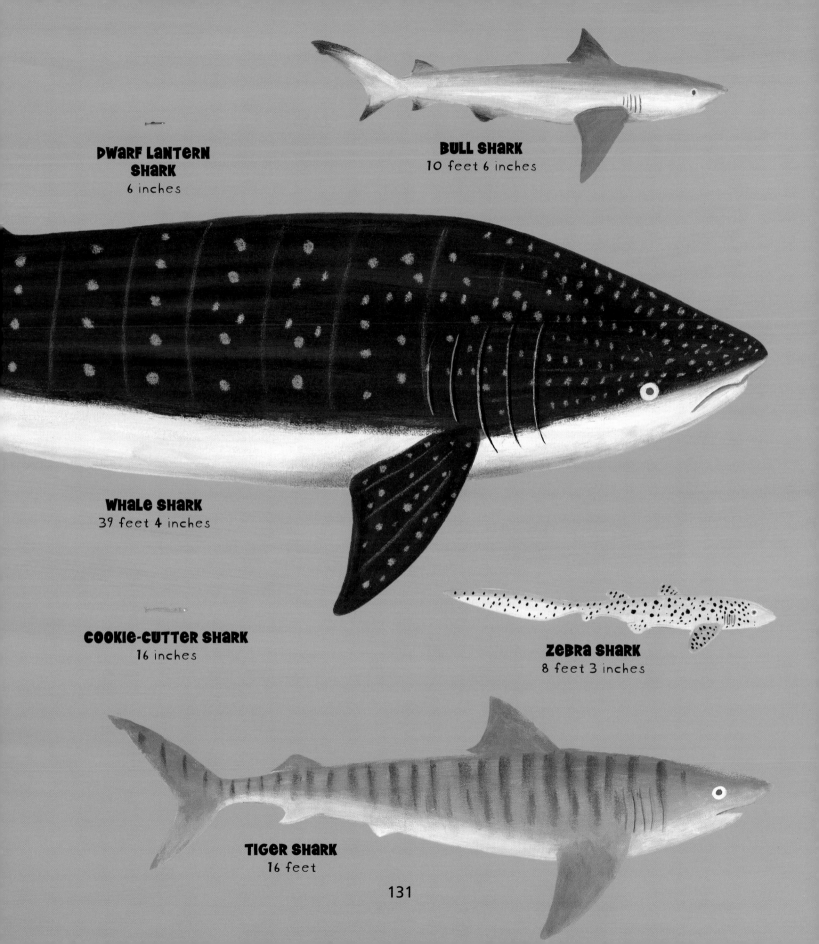

DWARF LANTERN SHARK
6 inches

BULL SHARK
10 feet 6 inches

WHALE SHARK
39 feet 4 inches

COOKIE-CUTTER SHARK
16 inches

ZEBRA SHARK
8 feet 3 inches

TIGER SHARK
16 feet

131

BLUE SHARK
10 feet 6 inches

BASKING SHARK
29 feet 6 inches

HAMMERHEAD SHARK
13 feet

MAKO SHARK
12 feet 8 inches

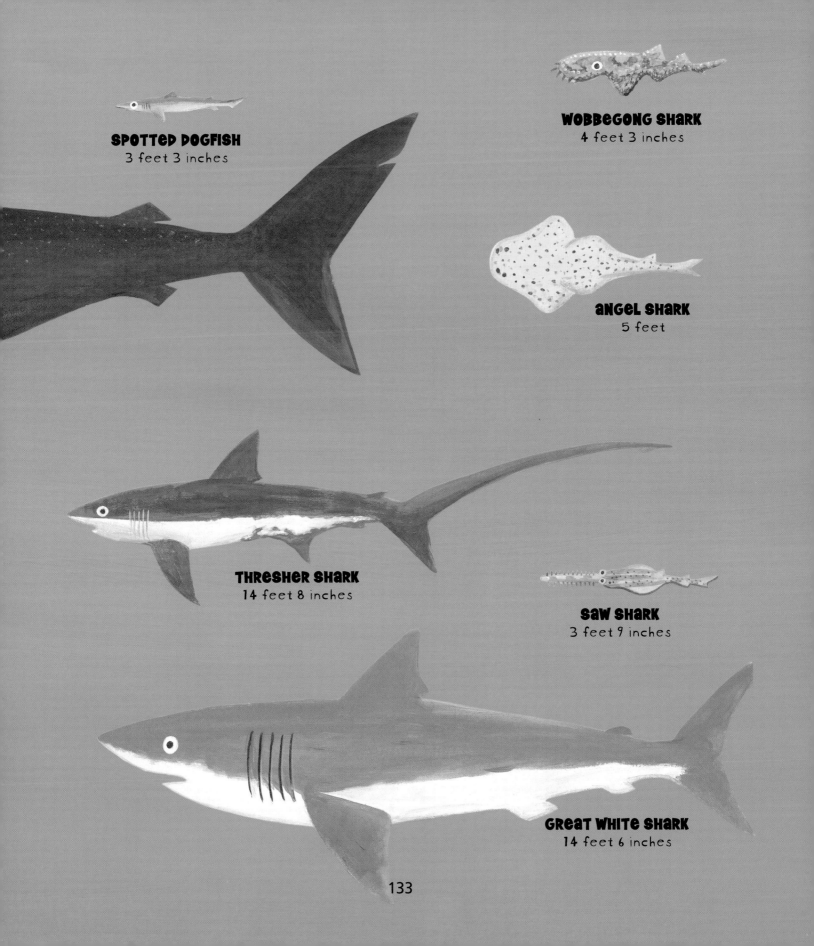

SPOTTED DOGFISH
3 feet 3 inches

WOBBEGONG SHARK
4 feet 3 inches

ANGEL SHARK
5 feet

THRESHER SHARK
14 feet 8 inches

SAW SHARK
3 feet 9 inches

GREAT WHITE SHARK
14 feet 6 inches

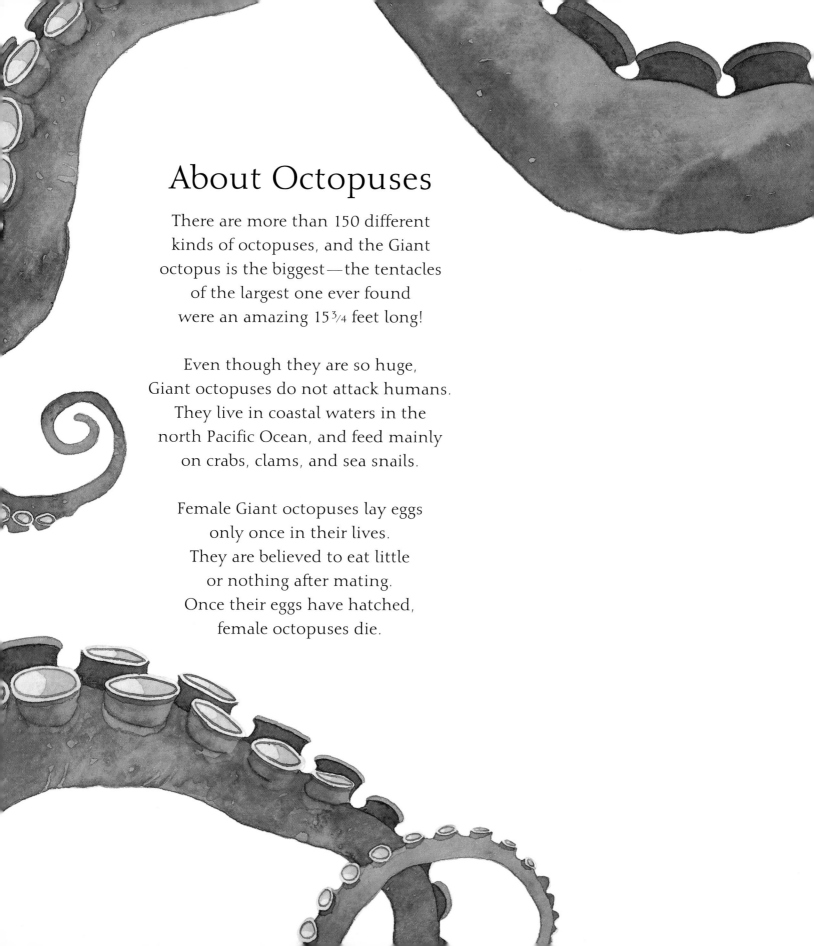

About Octopuses

There are more than 150 different
kinds of octopuses, and the Giant
octopus is the biggest—the tentacles
of the largest one ever found
were an amazing 15 $\frac{3}{4}$ feet long!

Even though they are so huge,
Giant octopuses do not attack humans.
They live in coastal waters in the
north Pacific Ocean, and feed mainly
on crabs, clams, and sea snails.

Female Giant octopuses lay eggs
only once in their lives.
They are believed to eat little
or nothing after mating.
Once their eggs have hatched,
female octopuses die.

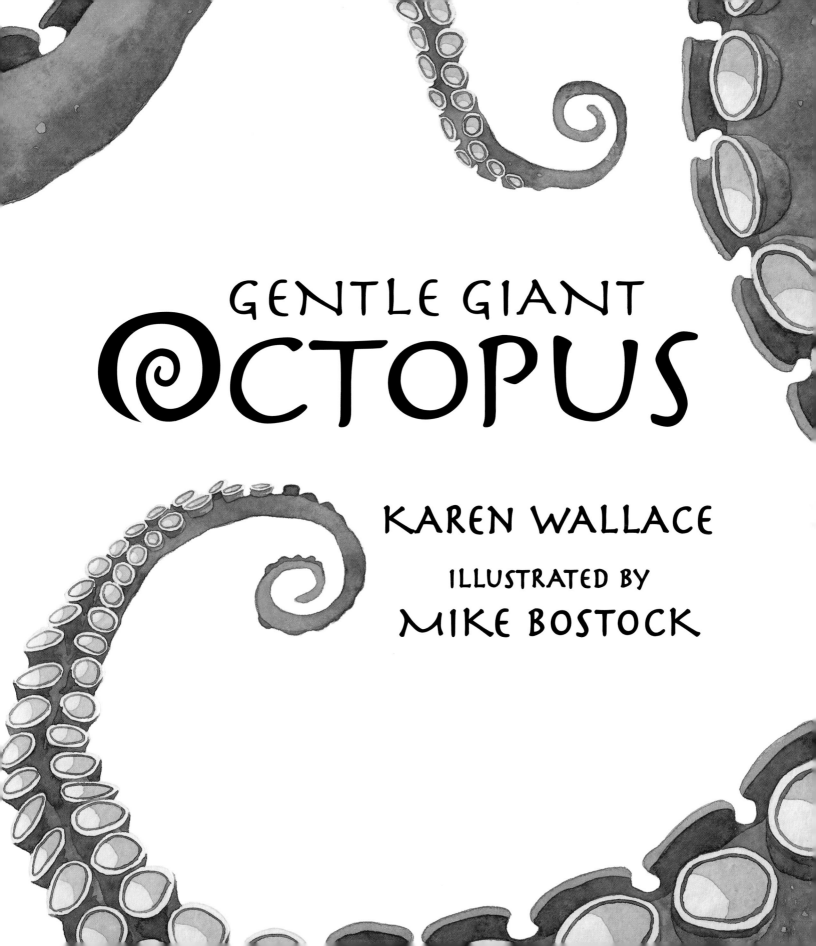

GENTLE GIANT
OCTOPUS

KAREN WALLACE

ILLUSTRATED BY
MIKE BOSTOCK

A gentle Giant octopus
jets through the shadows.
She's like a huge spaceship.
Her eyes glow in the water.
Long tentacles fly like
ribbons behind her.
Silver-backed fish
scatter before her.

A wandering mother octopus
moves through the water.
Inside her body, she carries her eggs.
She looks for a den that is safe
and well hidden,
for a crack in a rock face or
a hole under a stone.

When octopuses need to move quickly,

they jet backward by sucking in seawater

and pumping it out through a funnel-like siphon.

An octopus sinks
like a huge
rubber flower.

Sand muddies the water
as she lands on
the seabed.

Octopuses use their tentacles like fingers to sense things.

They use the suckers on their tentacles to grip things.

Octopus eyes turn
frontward and backward.
Her tentacles sense
a crab in the water.
A tentacle searches.
It stretches
and touches. . .

Unlucky
octopus!

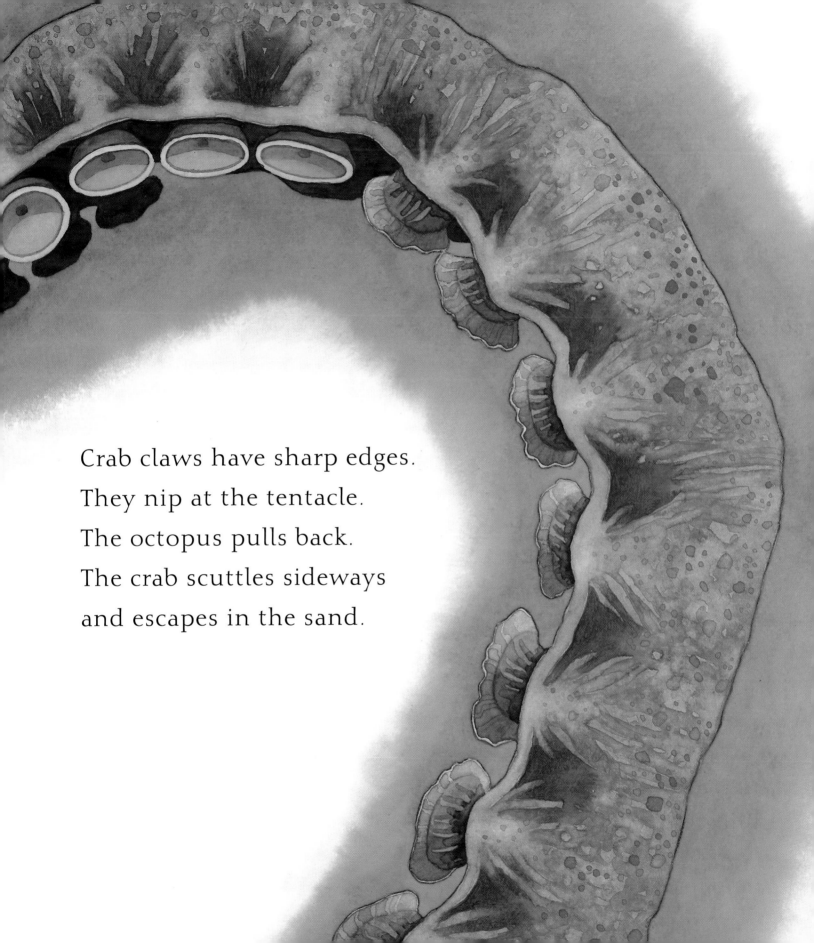

Crab claws have sharp edges.
They nip at the tentacle.
The octopus pulls back.
The crab scuttles sideways
and escapes in the sand.

A mother Giant octopus
slides over the seabed.
Her body stretches like taffy
over the stones.
Her skin ripples like seaweed.
She's black as the sea kelp.
The goggle-eyed octopus
feels her way forward.

Usually, the Giant octopus is reddish
brown, but when it's hunting or hiding,
it can change to become very dark
or very pale within seconds.

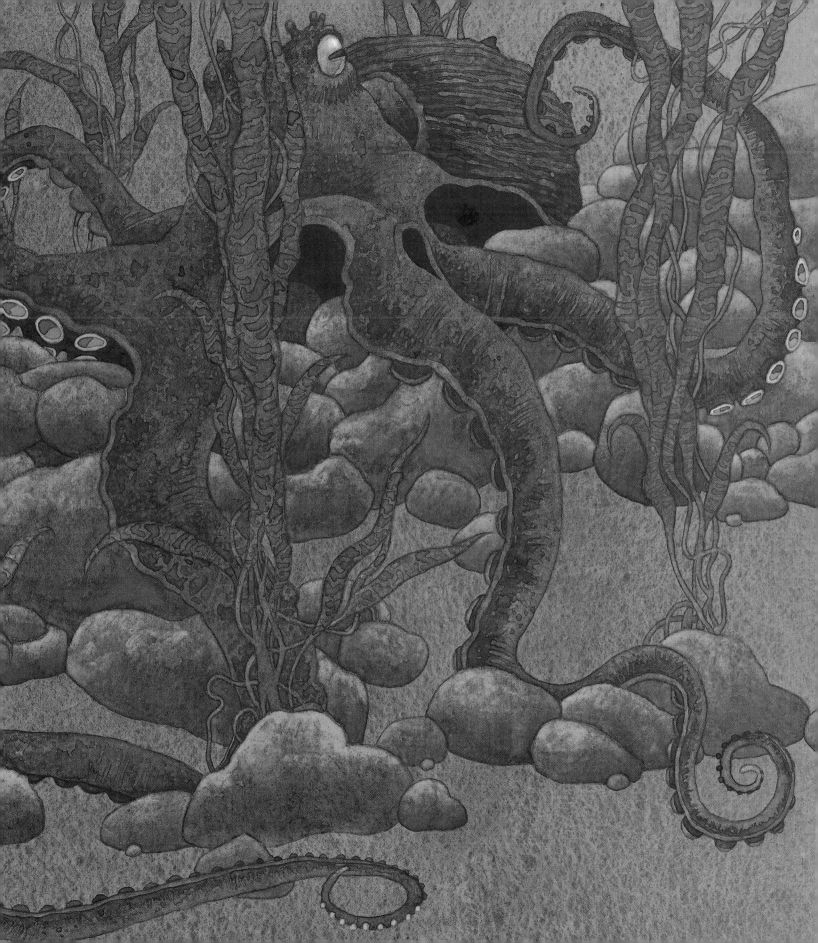

But under a boulder,
a wolf eel is waiting.
His mottled gray face darts
from the shadows.
His teeth strike
like daggers.
He rips off
a tentacle . . . .

Octopuses have eight tentacles. A healthy octopus can regrow its tentacles if they are damaged.

then sinks
like a nightmare
deep into his den.

149

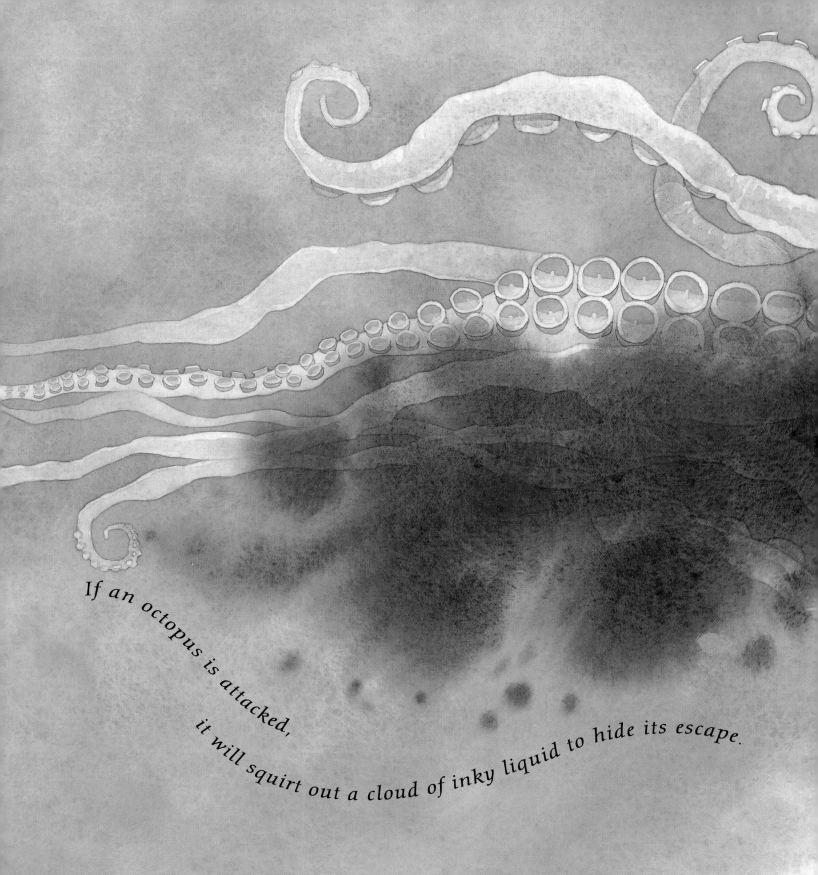

If an octopus is attacked, it will squirt out a cloud of inky liquid to hide its escape.

A frightened Giant octopus
squirts ink at the wolf eel.
She shoots back from the boulder,
back over the seabed.
She's pumping and sucking
the sea from her body.

A quivering Giant octopus
rests on a boulder.

Underneath is a cave
that is easily guarded.

Octopuses are about as clever as cats—and like cats, they're very curious.

She squeezes inside.
She drags pebbles around her.

Her search for a home
is over at last.

Octopuses don't have any bones, and they can squeeze through the tiniest of holes.

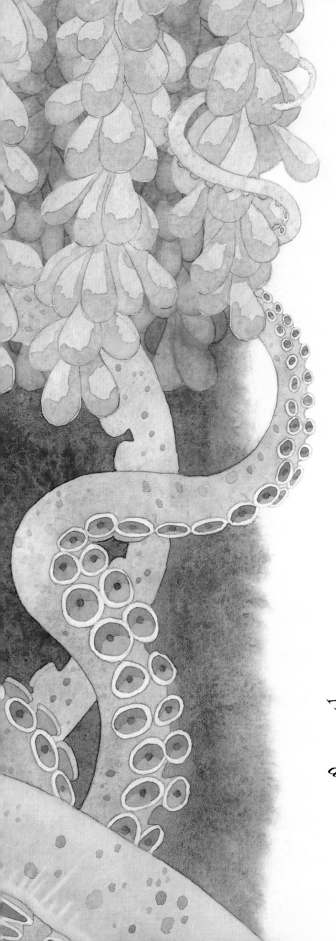

A mother Giant octopus lays
eggs in her cave den.
They hang from the roof
like grapes on a string.
She guards them from crabs
and nibbling fishes.
While her babies are growing,
she never eats and never rests.

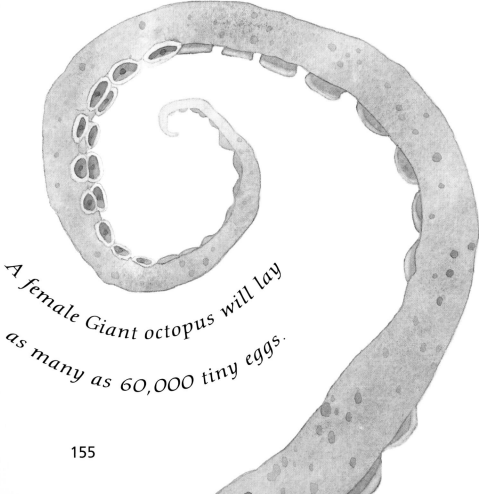

A female Giant octopus will lay
as many as 60,000 tiny eggs.

After five months, her babies
swim from their egg sacs.
They squirm and they wiggle.
They jet through the shadows.
They're sucking and pumping
the sea from their bodies.

Lots of other animals like to eat baby octopuses, so only two or three out of every brood live to become adults.

A mother Giant octopus
rests in her cave den.
She watches her babies
swim up through
the water.

A gentle Giant octopus
shrinks in the shadows.
Her life is over as their lives begin.

About Polar Bears

By international agreement, polar bears are protected wherever they roam. But global warming may be melting the sea ice they depend on. Here are some things you can do to help preserve the polar bear's Arctic home:

- Switch off lights, televisions, and computers when you don't need them.
- Bike or walk instead of getting in the car.

Every little bit helps!

ICE BEAR

Nicola Davies

illustrated by
Gary Blythe

IN THE STEPS OF THE POLAR BEAR

Polar bears have longer necks and legs than their closest relatives—brown or grizzly bears.

OUR people, the Inuit, call it NANUK.

White bear, ice bear, sea bear, others say.

It's a bear, all right, but not like any other!

It's a POLAR BEAR, made for our frozen world!

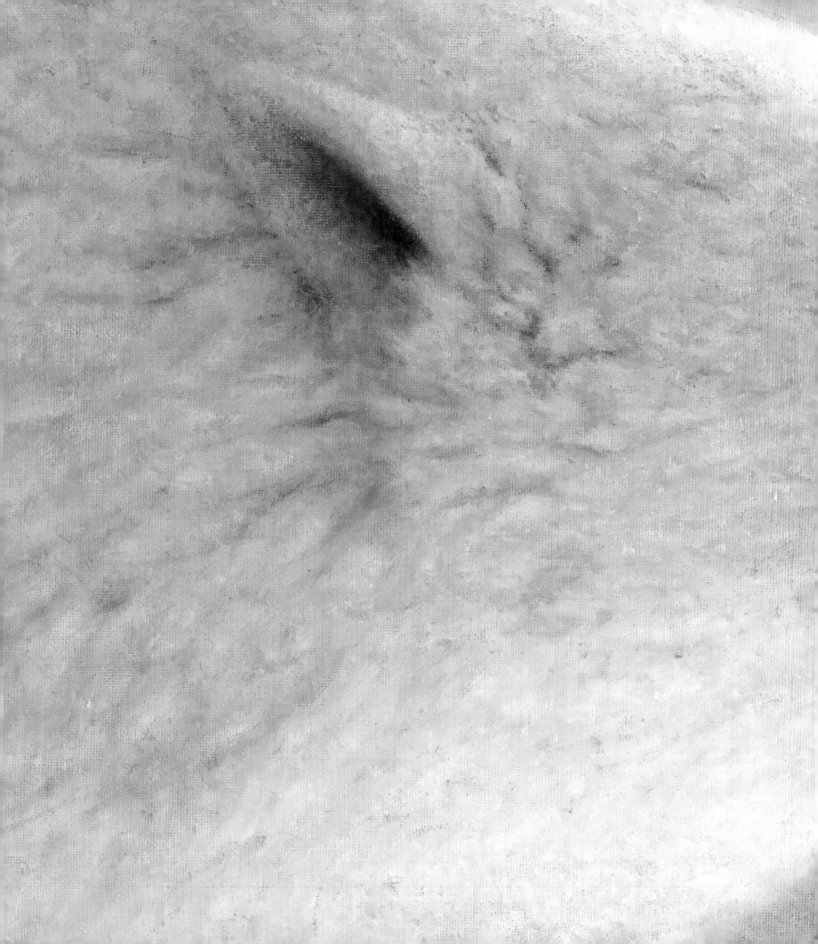

No frost can steal **POLAR BEAR**'s heat. It has a double coat: one of fat, four fingers deep, and one of fur, which has an extra trick for beating cold. Its hairs aren't really white, but hollow, filled with air, to stop the warmth from escaping, and underneath, the skin is black to soak up heat.

Only a polar bear's nose and the pads on the ends of its toes are without fur.

Tiny ice crystals rub the dirt from the polar bear's fur.

Polar bears are careful to keep clean so that they stay camouflaged against the snow and ice.

Its ears sit close to its head,

neatly out of cutting winds,

and its feet are furred for warmth

and grip. So **POLAR BEAR**

stays warm no matter what.

It will sleep away a blizzard in a drift,

and wash in snow.

Polar bears stay warm in temperatures of minus 40°F and lower.

167

POLAR BEAR is a great hunter.
It outweighs two lions
and makes a tiger look small.

Polar bears are the biggest hunters on land. Male bears can be 10 feet long and weigh as much as ten men.

A single paw would fill this page—
and shred the paper with its claws.

It can run as fast as a snowmobile
or walk and walk for days on end.
It can swim a hundred miles without a rest
to cross the sea between the ice floes,
then shake the water from its fur and walk again.

Polar bears' fat keeps them warm in the cold sea.

Webbed feet help them to swim,
and water-shedding fur helps them dry off quickly afterward.

Nothing stops POLAR BEAR.

Polar bears can catch seals only on the sea ice, so hunting is best in winter and early spring.

Seals are its prey.

It hunts them far out on the frozen sea,

waiting at a breathing hole

or stalking them as they sleep.

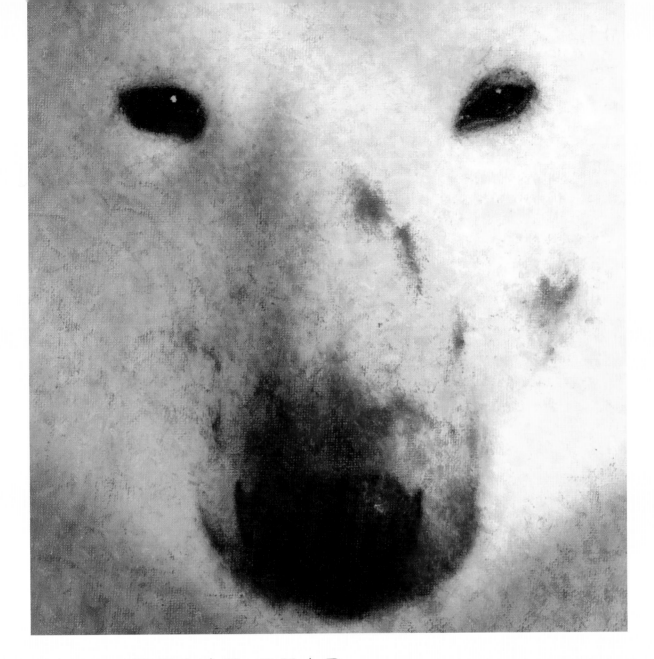

POLAR BEAR is a white shape
in a white world, invisible until it's too late.
A lightning paw strike, a crushing bite,
and the seal is gone.

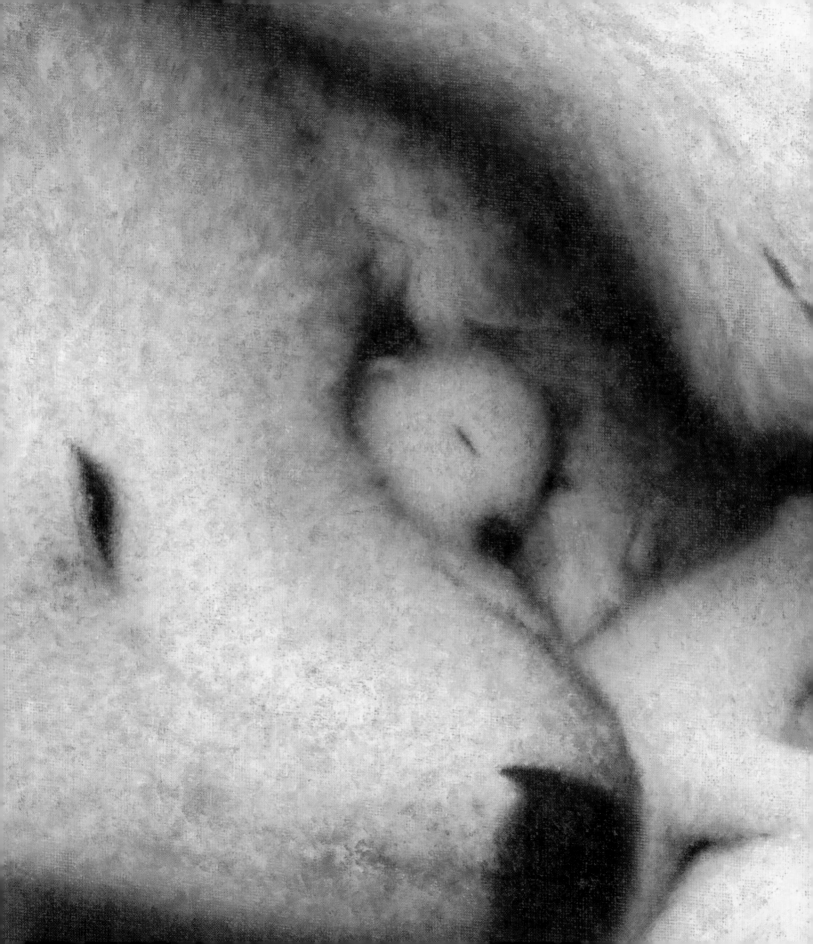

But **POLAR BEAR**

is gentle too.

Mother Polar Bear, in her

winter snow den,

tends her newborn cubs.

She lifts their tiny bodies

in her great paws

and suckles them.

Newborn polar bears are tiny.
They weigh just over one pound—about the same as a guinea pig!

175

In spring, she'll take them hunting,
and for two years she'll protect and feed them,
until they've learned, like her,
to hunt . . . alone.

Polar bear moms usually have two cubs at a time, but sometimes they have only one or, very rarely, triplets.

ALONE . . . through summers, when the sun
tracks up and down the sky and one day
passes to another with no night between.

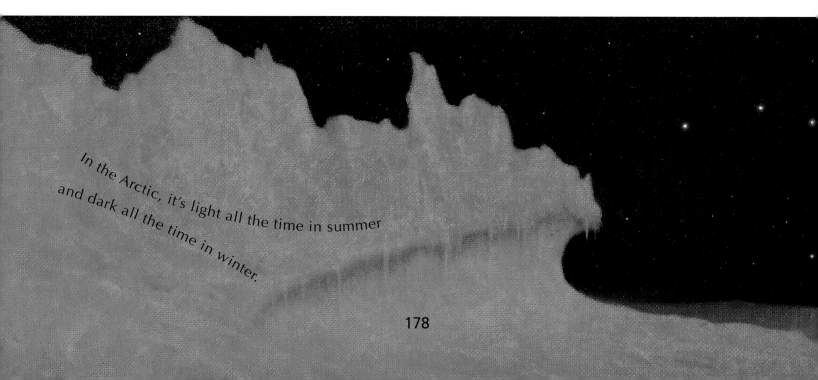

In the Arctic, it's light all the time in summer
and dark all the time in winter.

When the sea ice melts in summer, polar bears can't catch seals. They'll eat almost anything instead: fish, dead birds, berries, and even grass.

ALONE ... through winters, when the sun never rises and the stars of the Great Bear sparkle in the darkness.

ALONE . . . until the paths
of two lone hunters cross.
They'll wave their heads in
greeting, clasp jaws so tenderly,
they wouldn't break an egg.
Cautiously, they'll try each
other's strength.

Then? Play!

Giants flowing in the
whiteness, tumbling,
beautiful as snowflakes . . .

Real fighting is very dangerous for polar bears!
So males play-fight to find out who's the strongest
without either bear getting hurt.

Some scientists think that when humans came to the Arctic around 40,000 years ago, they learned how to survive by watching polar bears.

until they part and slowly go their separate ways.

WE Inuit, we watch NANUK,
as we first watched when the Earth seemed new
and POLAR BEAR showed us
how to love the Arctic—
how to hide from blizzards in a house of snow,
how to hunt for seals with patience and with speed,
how to live in starlit day and sunlit night.

Many polar bears and Inuit have passed since then,
and still we share our world with gratitude and pride.

INDEX

About the Authors

Martin Jenkins is a conservation biologist and author of the award-winning *The Emperor's Egg*. The first time he saw wild elephants was in Kenya. "There was a big family of them making their way across the savanna," he says. "I'll never forget them, strolling across the plains. It was magic."

Octopuses have a special place in Karen Wallace's imagination, from the storybook monsters of folklore to the young octopus she watched escape from a fish trap and back to the safety of the sea. Her many picture books include *Think of an Eel*, which won a Parents' Choice Award.

Nicola Davies is a zoologist and writer with a special love of the sea. She has seen basking sharks off the coast of England and has studied whales in the open ocean. But it's not just the ocean that intrigues her: "The Far North has a firm hold on me!" she says, which explains her love of polar bears.

Nick Dowson is a teacher and writer. He loves wild places and the animals that live there, like the tiger and the panda. "Mountains are where I like to be the most," he says, "just like the giant panda."

About the Illustrators

Ivan Bates has illustrated a number of children's books. *About Grandma Elephant's in Charge*, he says, "I have always found elephants fascinating creatures, capable of both extreme strength and tenderness. This, combined with their almighty stature ... makes them a joy to draw."

Gary Blythe has illustrated several picture books for children, but this is his first nonfiction title. The majesty of the polar bears provided him with lots of inspiration as well as the chance to work with a whole new range of bright colors.

Mike Bostock became fascinated by octopuses while illustrating this book—the delicate, changing color and texture of their skin; the rubbery, rippling way they move; and their transparent soap bubble–like babies.

Yu Rong studied Chinese art in Nanjing before moving to London, where she received a master's degree from the Royal College of Art. "Panda and I have the same nationality," she says, "and I have a very deep love for pandas."

James Croft has always enjoyed drawing sharks. Their teeth and speed as well as the sense of danger they evoke have fueled his imagination like no other creature. James Croft lives and works in London.

Jane Chapman is the award-winning illustrator of many books, including *The Emperor's Egg*. She thinks that tiger mothers must have a tough time in India's warm climate. "I would be so grumpy in all that heat," she says. "No wonder they spend so much time in the water!"

Nick Maland began drawing while pursuing a career in acting. "I have illustrated for many newspapers and magazines, but it was not until my daughter, Eloise, was born that I turned to children's books".

NOTES FOR TEACHERS

The READ AND WONDER series is an innovative and versatile resource for reading, thinking, and discovery. Each book invites children to become excited about a topic, see how varied information books can be, and want to find out more.

☞ **Reading aloud.** The story form makes these books ideal for reading aloud — their own or as part of a cross-curricular topic, to a child or to a whole class. After you've introduced children to the books in this way, they can revisit and enjoy them again and again.

☞ **Shared reading.** Big Book editions are available for several titles that so children can read along, discuss the topic, and comment on the different ways information is presented — to wonder together.

☞ **Group and guided reading.** Children need to experience a range of reading materials. Information books like these help develop the skills of reading to learn as part of learning to read. With the support of a reading group, children can become confident, flexible readers.

☞ **Paired reading.** It's fun to take turns to read the information in the main text or in the captions. With a partner, children can explore the pages to satisfy their curiosity and build their understanding.

☞ **Individual reading.** These books can be read for interest and pleasure by children at home or in school.

☞ **Research** Once children have been introduced to these books through reading aloud, they can use them for independent or group research, as part of a curricular topic.

☞ **Children's own writing.** You can offer these books as strong models for children's own information writing. They can record their observations and findings about a topic, make field notes and sketches, and add extra snippets of information for the reader.

Above all, Read and Wonders are to be enjoyed, encouraging children to develop a lasting curiosity about the world they live in.

Sue Ellis, Centre for Literacy in Primary Education, London, United Kingdom